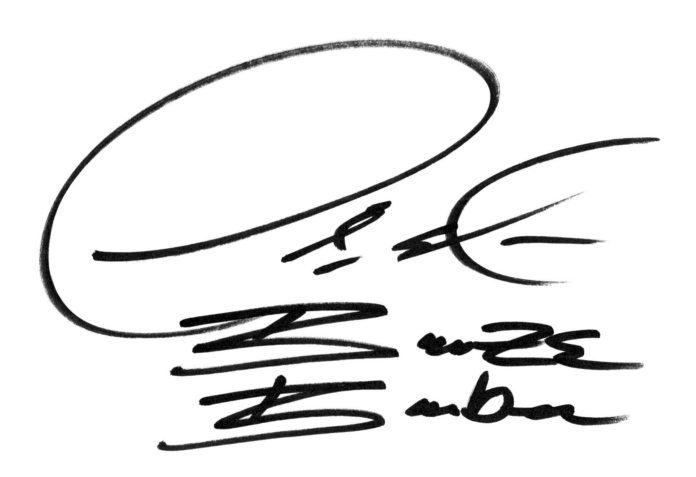

Deontay
The Future
World Champ!

A story inspired by the true life of
World Heavyweight Champion Deontay Wilder

Written by

Tony Bowers

Illustrated by

Dan Monroe

Library of Congress Control Number: 2014910189

ISBN 978-0-9960374-2-6

First edition hardcover

Published by:
PencilWerk Press
P.O. Box 452
Paw Paw, Mi 49079

www.pencilwerkpress.com

Written by Tony Bowers

Based on the true-life events of
World Heavyweight Champion
Deontay Wilder aka "The Bronze Bomber"

Art and illustrations copyright © 2014 Dan Monroe

Edited by Ashley Monroe

Printed in the United States of America

This book is dedicated to the two loves of my life.
Karizma and Kloie my two beautiful girls,you are angels that walk amongst us in this world.
Reach for the stars and beyond that,never be satisfied were you are at.
Don't just get by live your life everyday, try to make this world better in your own way.
Everything I do is to make you two proud of me.
I love you girls

I would also like,to thank Lauren Garthe.
Thank you for believing in me when I didn't believe in myself.

Gone but never forgotten:

My father Wayne j Bowers
Mrs.A
Matthew Soriano aka Zero

We love and miss you

-Tony Bowers

The illustrations in this book are dedicated to people of all ages, everywhere, who have a passion - Strive daily to fulfill it, no matter what. Through your hard work, dedication, and persistance you will achieve your dreams.

And to my wife and children for believing in me always though others tried to beat me down.

Remain True to Yourself Always!

-Dan Monroe

On a hot summer day perfect to play,
all the kids were, but not Deontay.

Deontay jogged away. The kids started to shout,
"World Champ?...Ha ha ha! Deontay's missing out!"

Deontay kept on training then Kevin came running,
"Everybody come quick the ice cream man is coming!"

They all got ice cream and started licking away,
all the kids did, but not Deontay.

"Would you like some ice cream?" the ice cream man said. Deontay smiled at him and then shook his head.

"Why not Deontay? I have everything you need, sprinkles, chocolate syrup, and even whipped cream."

"I wish that I could but right now I can't,
I'm training real hard to be the World Champ!"

The kids started to laugh, then started to scream,
"Why would you train when you can eat ice cream?"

Deontay jogged away and saw Laurie and Kate.
"Hey Deontay, why not take a break?"

"The fair is in town, we can go on the rides, eat cotton candy, and race down the slides!"

Deontay jogged away. Laurie waved goodbye.
He went to the gym and started to cry.

Coach Jay asked "Deontay, are you okay? Why are you crying on this beautiful day?"

"I wish I could swim, and go on the rides, eat ice cream, and race down the slides."

"Like the rest of my friends having all the fun.
The only thing I get to do is run."

Coach Jay wiped away Deontays tears,
"There's no need to cry,
I know how you feel."

"You work so hard each and every day,
why wouldn't you want to go outside and play?"

"The road to World Champ like I told you before, is gonna take hard work and a little bit more."

"Ice cream and candy are a great treat, but fruits and nuts are just as sweet."

"Eating right and training will keep your body strong,
because the road to World Champ is gonna be long."

Later that day the kids in town had a race.
Coach Jay said "Deontay go get in your place."

They started to run, but half of the way,
the kids were all tired, but not Deontay.

Deontay won the race in record time,
and gave Coach Jay a "high five"
when he crossed the finish line.

"Eating right and training is why I won the race,
the other kids were all tired from the food that they ate."

Now the kids wave when Deontay jogs by,
and if someone asks, "Hey who's that little guy?"

About the Author

Born in Queens, NY, Tony Bowers began writing in the 3rd grade. With help from his teacher, he started a subscription based comic book series; "Super Tony", which he sold to his classmates. Tony later started writing screenplays, songs, and story boards for music videos. While pursuing a career in music, he was blessed to father two beautiful daughters. He soon realized that music and traveling was taking too much time away from his family. Tony decided to return to his roots as a children's book author. He has since released several books for children, including one based on his daughter. This book is titled "Kloie and the Magic Bookmark" and is being turned into an animated cartoon series. Tony also visits local schools in an effort to help promote literacy.

To contact Tony Bowers:

tonyteflon1@gmail.com

About the Artist

Michigan based artist Dan Monroe has been creating illustrations and works of art for over thirty years. His work has been exhibited and sold in art galleries across the country, and he taught art at Western Michigan University. From his early days learning airbrush techniques in the street markets of Hawaii, to formal classes at Kendall College, he has honed his craft, working as illustrator on a number of creative projects, including illustrating children's books for such celebrities as Dennis Rodman, former "Baywatch" actress Erika Eleniak, and actor Robert Rusler, who starred in "Weird Science" and was a regular on the sci-fi cult TV show "Babylon 5". His works have been featured on "The Tonight Show" with Jay Leno, "The Late Show" with Jimmy Fallon, the Oprah Winfrey Network, and in media around the world. Dan lives with his wife Lori, their children, and their cat - Thor.

To contact Dan Monroe:

    d.monroe@dragonbrusher.com

Magic Treasure Books is a division of PencilWerk Press.

For any information concerning this book please write to:

info@pencilwerkpress.com